EXPOSED! MYTHS ABOUT EARLY AMERICAN HISTORY

THOMAS JEFFERSON DIDN'T SIGN THE CONSTITUTION

EXPOSING MYTHS ABOUT THE CONSTITUTIONAL CONVENTION

BY BARBARA M. LINDE

Gareth Stevens PUBLISHING

Please visit our website, www.garethstevens.com. For a free color catalog of all our high-quality books, call toll free 1-800-542-2595 or fax 1-877-542-2596.

Cataloging-in-Publication Data

Names: Linde, Barbara M.
Title: Thomas Jefferson didn't sign the Constitution : exposing myths about the Constitutional Convention/ Barbara M. Linde.
Description: New York : Gareth Stevens Publishing, 2017. | Series: Exposed! myths about early American history | Includes index.
Identifiers: ISBN 9781482457353 (pbk.) | ISBN 9781482457377 (library bound) | ISBN 9781482457360 (6 pack)
Subjects: LCSH: United States. Constitution–Juvenile literature. | Constitutional history–Juvenile literature. | United States. Constitutional Convention, 1787–Juvenile literature.
Classification: LCC KF4550.Z9 L56 2017 | DDC 342.7302'9–dc23

First Edition

Published in 2017 by
Gareth Stevens Publishing
111 East 14th Street, Suite 349
New York, NY 10003

Designer: Sarah Liddell
Editor: Therese Shea

Photo credits: Cover, p. 1 (background image) Superstock/Getty Images; cover, pp. 1 (Thomas Jefferson), 23 (James Madison) GraphicaArtis/Contributor/Archive Photos/Getty Images; background texture used throughout IS MODE/Shutterstock.com; ripped newspaper used throughout STILLFX/Shutterstock.com; photo corners used throughout Carolyn Franks/Shutterstock.com; pp. 5, 15 Visions of America/Contributor/ Universal Images Group/Getty Images; p. 7 Forgottendelights/Wikimedia Commons; p. 9 (Washington) Dcoetzee/Wikimedia Commons; p. 9 (voting record) Denniss/Wikimedia Commons; p. 11 Bettman/ Contributor/Bettman/Getty Images; p. 13 Stock Montage/Contributor/Archive Photos/Getty Images; p. 17 (15th Amendment) Keeleysam/Wikimedia Commons; p. 17 (main) JEWEL SAMAD/Staff/AFP/ Getty Images; p. 19 (both), 23 (top) photos courtesy of National Archives; p. 21 Joseph Sohm/ Shutterstock.com; p. 25 (Jonathan Dayton) File Upload Bot (Magnis Manske)/Wikimedia Commons; p. 25 (Constitution signatures) Drdpw/Wikimedia Commons; p. 27 (John Jay) Scewing/Wikimedia Commons; p. 27 (James Madison) Botaurus/Wikimedia Commons; p. 27 (Alexander Hamilton) Hohum/ Wikimedia Commons; p. 27 (Patrick Henry) Complex01/Wikimedia Commons; p. 27 (James Monroe) Maximilian Schönherr/Wikimedia Commons; p. 27 (Sam Adams) Harpsichord246/Wikimedia Commons; p. 29 MarshalN20/WIkimedia Commons.

Printed in China

CPSIA compliance information: Batch #CW17GS: For further information contact Gareth Stevens, New York, New York at 1-800-542-2595.

CONTENTS

The Constitution of the United States 4

At the Constitutional Convention 6

Who Was There? 10

What's in There, and What's Not 14

The "Father of the Constitution"? 22

The Magic Number 24

After the Convention 26

Glossary 30

For More Information 31

Index 32

Words in the glossary appear in **bold** type the first time they are used in the text.

THE CONSTITUTION OF THE UNITED STATES

On September 17 of each year, Americans honor Constitution Day. They remember the day in 1787 that a group of state **representatives** met in Philadelphia, Pennsylvania, to sign the **document** they had created: the US Constitution. The Constitution is the document that describes the American government and the basic laws of the country.

Over the years, **myths** have replaced some of the facts about the Constitutional **Convention** and the amazing document itself. Let's look at some of them.

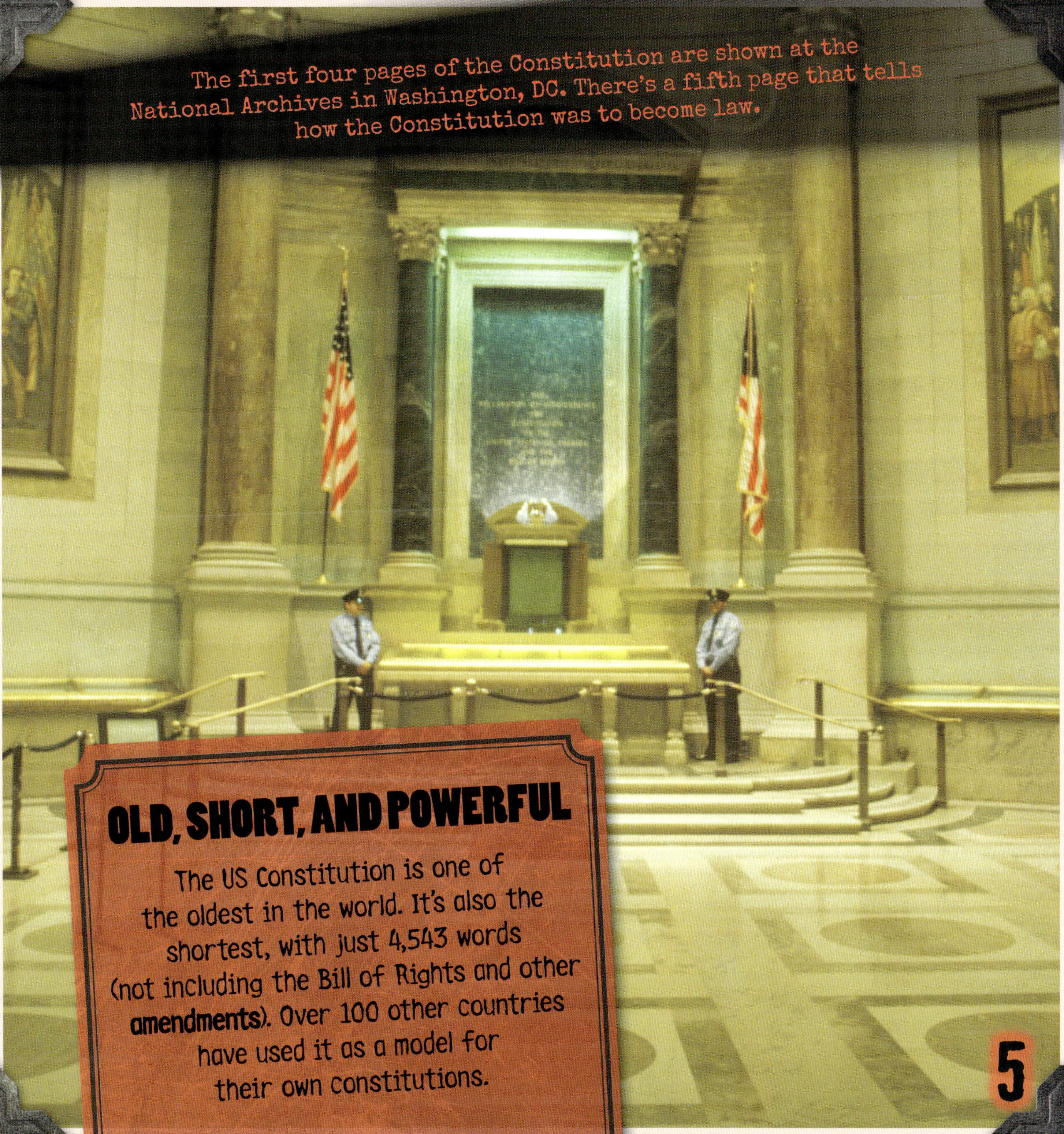

The first four pages of the Constitution are shown at the National Archives in Washington, DC. There's a fifth page that tells how the Constitution was to become law.

OLD, SHORT, AND POWERFUL

The US Constitution is one of the oldest in the world. It's also the shortest, with just 4,543 words (not including the Bill of Rights and other **amendments**). Over 100 other countries have used it as a model for their own constitutions.

AT THE CONSTITUTIONAL CONVENTION

Before the US Constitution went into effect, the 13 states used a set of laws called the Articles of Confederation. It didn't work well. The national government had little power. So the country's leaders met in 1787 to fix the Articles. But they soon realized they needed new laws and a stronger federal, or central, government.

They worked from May to September, through the hot summer. They kept the Pennsylvania State House windows and doors shut for secrecy. After a lot of arguing, the Framers had created a new government.

THE FRAMERS

We call the men at the convention the "Framers" because they framed, or constructed, the Constitution. In notes and letters, the Framers talked of the terrible summer heat. In those days, men wore coats all day, sometimes made of wool.

These statues of the Framers are found at the National Constitution Center in Philadelphia, Pennsylvania.

THE MYTH: REPRESENTATIVES FROM ALL 13 ORIGINAL STATES HELPED WRITE THE US CONSTITUTION.

THE FACTS:

Only 12 of the 13 states sent delegates, or representatives, to the convention. Seventy men were chosen by their states, and 55 attended. The Framers were well-educated white men who owned land and were leaders in their own states.

Rhode Island was the one state that didn't send any delegates to the convention. Most of its people liked being independent. Rhode Islanders feared a stronger federal government would have too much power over their small state.

A MIRACLE?

George Washington wrote that the convention seemed "little short of a **miracle**." He was amazed that so many people with different points of view could come together to successfully create a new national government.

GEORGE WASHINGTON

This is the final vote on the Constitution from September 15, 1787. You can see that the column for Rhode Island's votes is empty. The New York column is blank as those delegates left early.

WHO WAS THERE?

THE MYTH:

ALL THE MEN WHO SIGNED THE DECLARATION OF INDEPENDENCE WERE ALSO AT THE CONSTITUTIONAL CONVENTION.

THE FACTS:

Not quite. Only six of the 56 Founding Fathers signed both documents. They were Benjamin Franklin, George Clymer, Robert Morris, George Read, Roger Sherman, and James Wilson.

John Adams was acting as US **ambassador** to Great Britain, so he couldn't sign. Massachusetts representative Caleb Strong went home when he disagreed with some of the decisions. Samuel Adams and John Hancock didn't attend the convention because they, too, worried a powerful new federal government would take away states' rights.

In this **engraving**, George Washington, president of the convention, is standing. Benjamin Franklin is sitting in the front row, and some of the other Framers are writing.

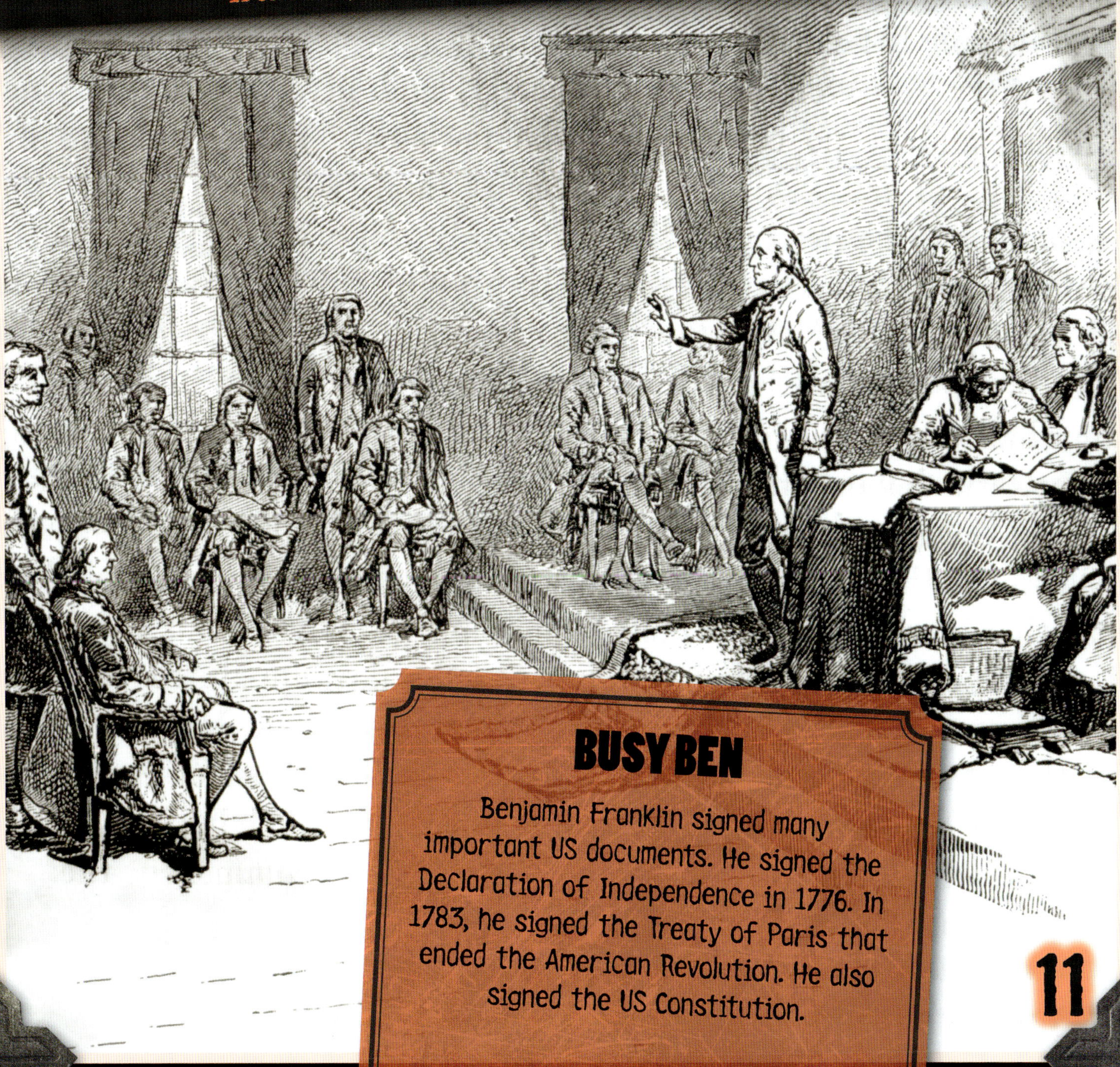

BUSY BEN

Benjamin Franklin signed many important US documents. He signed the Declaration of Independence in 1776. In 1783, he signed the Treaty of Paris that ended the American Revolution. He also signed the US Constitution.

THE MYTH: THOMAS JEFFERSON ATTENDED THE CONVENTION AND SIGNED THE CONSTITUTION.

THE FACTS:

Thomas Jefferson was an important American leader at the time of the convention. He had been the main writer of the Declaration of Independence and signed that document. Jefferson was in favor of a new constitution, but at that time, he was the US ambassador to France and living in Paris.

Jefferson and James Madison wrote letters to each other about the convention. At one point, Madison told the group, "I believe, that were that gentleman now on this floor, he would be for the adoption of this constitution."

Thomas Jefferson told James Madison that he believed a "bill of rights" should be added to the Constitution to protect, or guard, certain freedoms.

BOOKS FROM JEFFERSON

While Jefferson was in Paris, he sent books about laws and governments to his friend, James Madison. Madison used the books while helping to write the Constitution.

WHAT'S IN THERE, AND WHAT'S NOT

THE MYTH: SLAVERY WASN'T TALKED ABOUT AT THE CONSTITUTIONAL CONVENTION.

THE FACTS:

While some Framers were strongly against slavery, about 25 owned slaves. Slavery was important to the southern **economy**. In order to get southern delegates to support the Constitution, the Framers made **compromises**.

First, Congress couldn't ban the slave trade until 1808. Runaway slaves could be caught in the North and returned to the South. Last, three-fifths of the slave population would be counted as part of each state's population, so the southern states would have more representatives in government.

FREEDOM AT LAST

It's true that the words "slaves" and "slavery" weren't used in the original Constitution. However, the 13th Amendment, passed in 1865, ended the practice of slavery in all states.

Both the Declaration of Independence and the US Constitution were signed in the Assembly Room of the Pennsylvania State House. In 1824, people began to call the building "Independence Hall," a name it has held since.

THE MYTH: THE US CONSTITUTION GAVE EVERYONE THE RIGHT TO VOTE.

THE FACTS:

There isn't one word in the Constitution about who can vote. At that time, only white men who owned land were able to vote.

After a long time, every citizen did get the right to vote. The 15th Amendment, passed in 1870, gave African American men the right to vote. American women didn't get the right to vote until the 19th Amendment was passed in 1919. Native Americans weren't able to vote until 1924 (and some states didn't allow them to vote until years later).

VOTING AGE

Before 1971, a US citizen had to be 21 years old to vote. The 26th Amendment changed the voting age to 18.

States hold much power over who can vote. Even today, some states don't allow people in prison to vote.

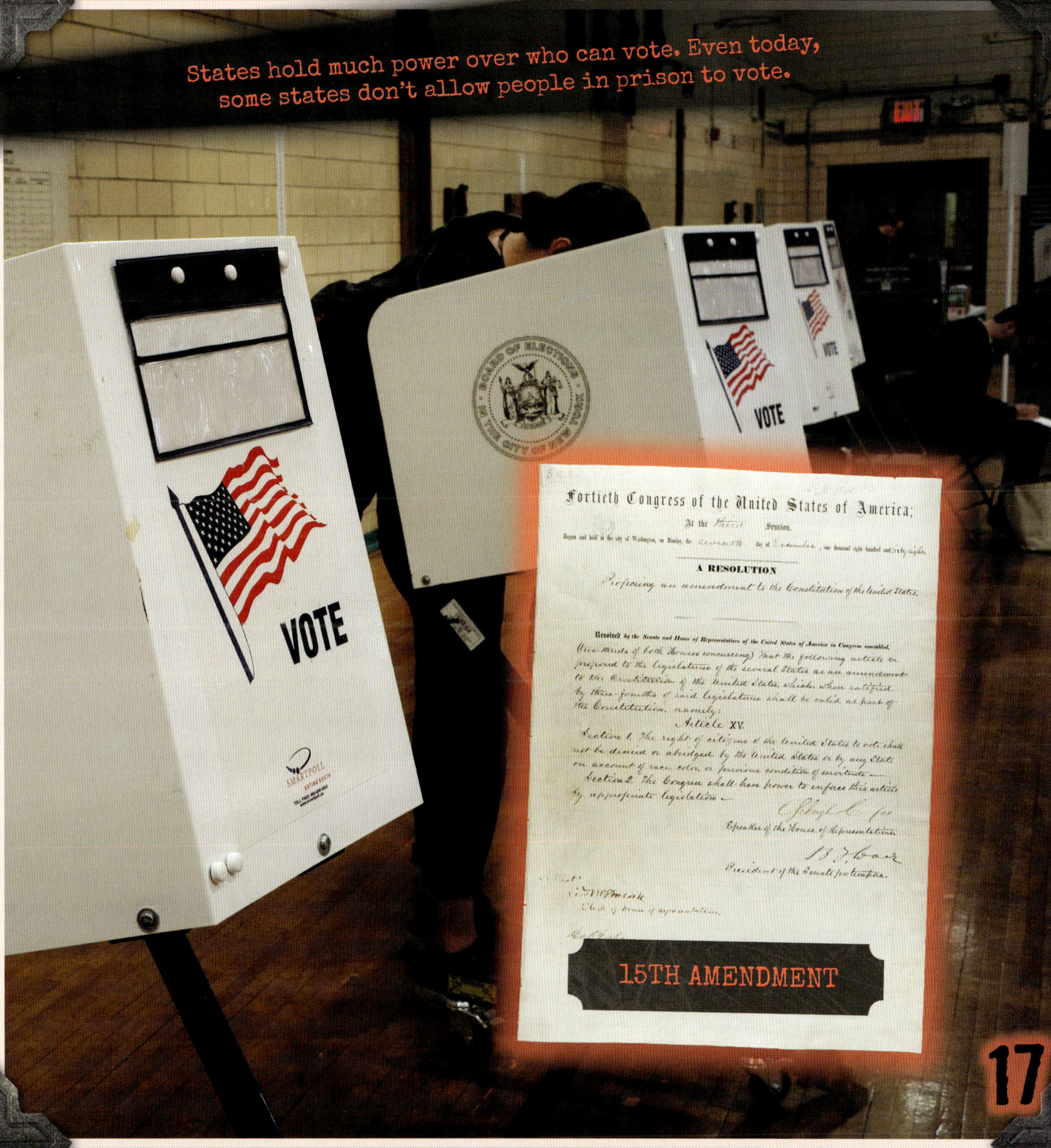

Fortieth Congress of the United States of America;

At the third Session.

Begun and held at the city of Washington, on Monday, the seventh day of December, one thousand eight hundred and sixty-eight.

A RESOLUTION

Proposing an amendment to the Constitution of the United States.

Resolved by the Senate and House of Representatives of the United States of America in Congress assembled, (two-thirds of both Houses concurring) that the following article be proposed to the legislatures of the several States as an amendment to the Constitution of the United States, which, when ratified by three-fourths of said legislatures shall be valid as part of the Constitution, namely:

Article XV.

Section 1. The right of citizens of the United States to vote shall not be denied or abridged by the United States or by any State on account of race, color, or previous condition of servitude—

Section 2. The Congress shall have power to enforce this article by appropriate legislation—

Speaker of the House of Representatives.

President of the Senate pro tempore.

Clerk of House of Representatives.

15TH AMENDMENT

THE MYTH: THE WORDS "ALL MEN ARE CREATED EQUAL" ARE IN THE US CONSTITUTION.

THE FACTS:

This is one of the most-believed myths about the Constitution, but it's not true. If these words sound familiar, they should. They're in the first part of the Declaration of Independence: "We hold these truths to be self-evident, that all men are created equal."

The famous opening of the Constitution is "We the People of the United States." This was actually a late change. At first, it read: "We the people of the States of New Hampshire, Massachusetts, ..." It listed every state!

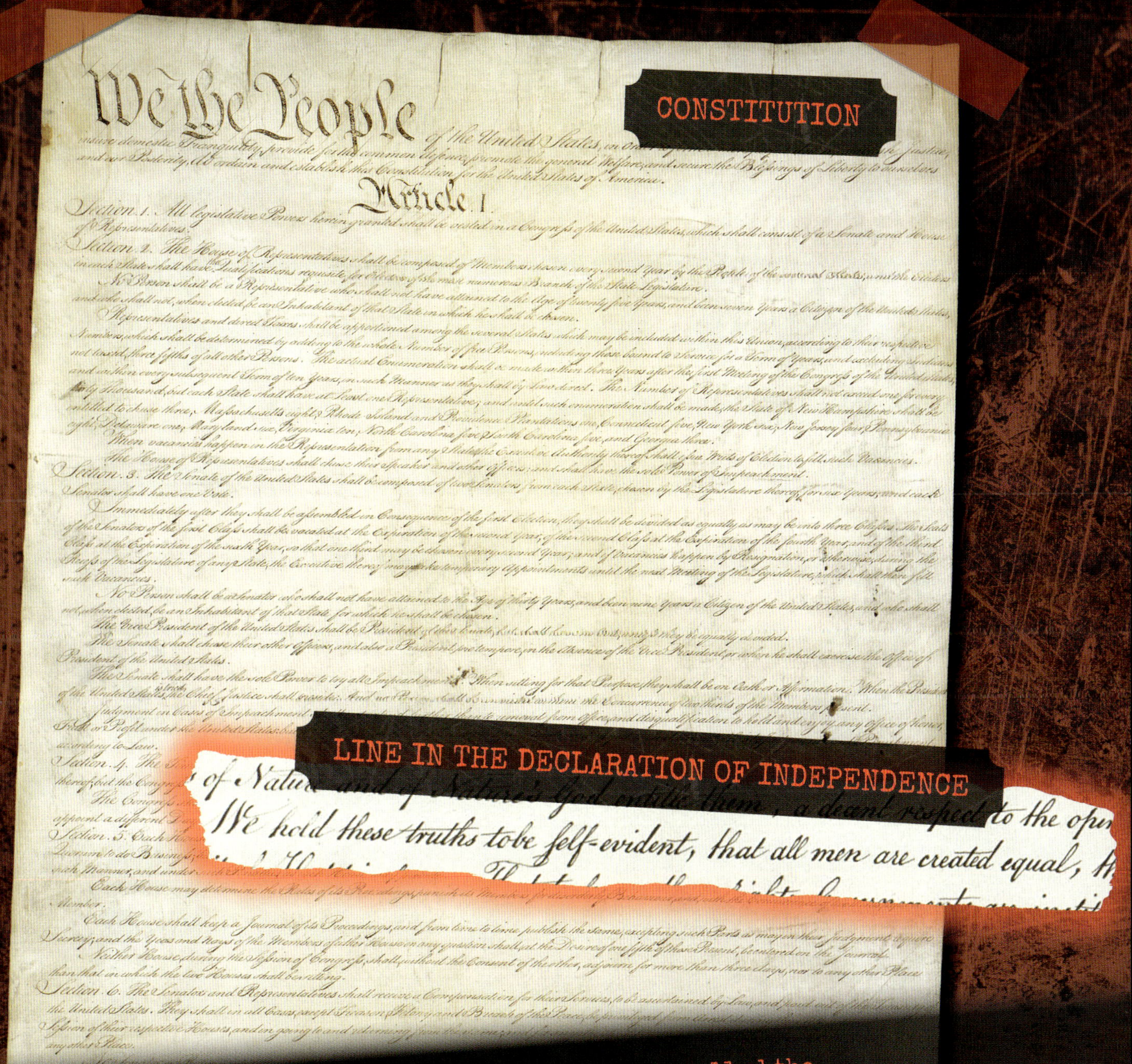

The first part of the Constitution is called the Preamble. You can see that the words "We the People" are written much larger than the rest of the words.

THE MYTH: THE US CONSTITUTION STATES THAT THE NATION IS A DEMOCRACY.

THE FACTS:

Article IV (4), Section 4, says: "The United States shall guarantee [promise] to every State in this Union a Republican Form of Government."

In a democracy, the majority always rules. People in the **minority** don't have a say. Their rights aren't protected. A republic usually protects everyone's freedoms with an official statement of rights, such as a constitution, so that no one person or group can get too powerful. In the republic created by the US Constitution, people vote for representatives to decide most matters in government.

When Americans say the Pledge of Allegiance, they say:
"I pledge allegiance to the flag of the United States of America,
and to the *Republic* for which it stands."

THE "FATHER OF THE CONSTITUTION"?

THE MYTH: JAMES MADISON IS THE "FATHER OF THE CONSTITUTION."

THE FACTS:

Madison's nickname started soon after the Constitution became law. It's a mix of myth and fact. James Madison studied other constitutions even before the convention. He created the Virginia Plan, which called for a strong central government made up of three branches. Much of his **proposal** was used in the Constitution. His notes of the convention were so exact that we still use them today.

But the Constitution wasn't his creation alone. The ideas of other Framers were also important.

This painting shows James Madison (second from left) handing the Constitution to George Washington.

JAMES MADISON

WHAT MADISON SAID

When asked if he was the "writer of the Constitution," James Madison said, "You give me a credit to which I have no claim." He stated that the Constitution "ought to be regarded as the work of many heads & many hands."

THE MAGIC NUMBER

THE MYTH: THIRTY-NINE MEN SIGNED THE CONSTITUTION.

THE FACTS:

This is tricky! Fifty-five Framers attended the meetings, but only 39 signed the Constitution. Some left to take care of other business. John Dickinson was sick, so George Read signed his name for him. George Mason, Edmund Randolph, and Elbridge Gerry were at the convention, but they didn't sign the document because it had no bill of rights.

William Jackson, the convention secretary, wasn't a delegate, but he signed the Constitution. So, the number of signers was 40.

This is the last page of the Constitution, which includes the signatures.

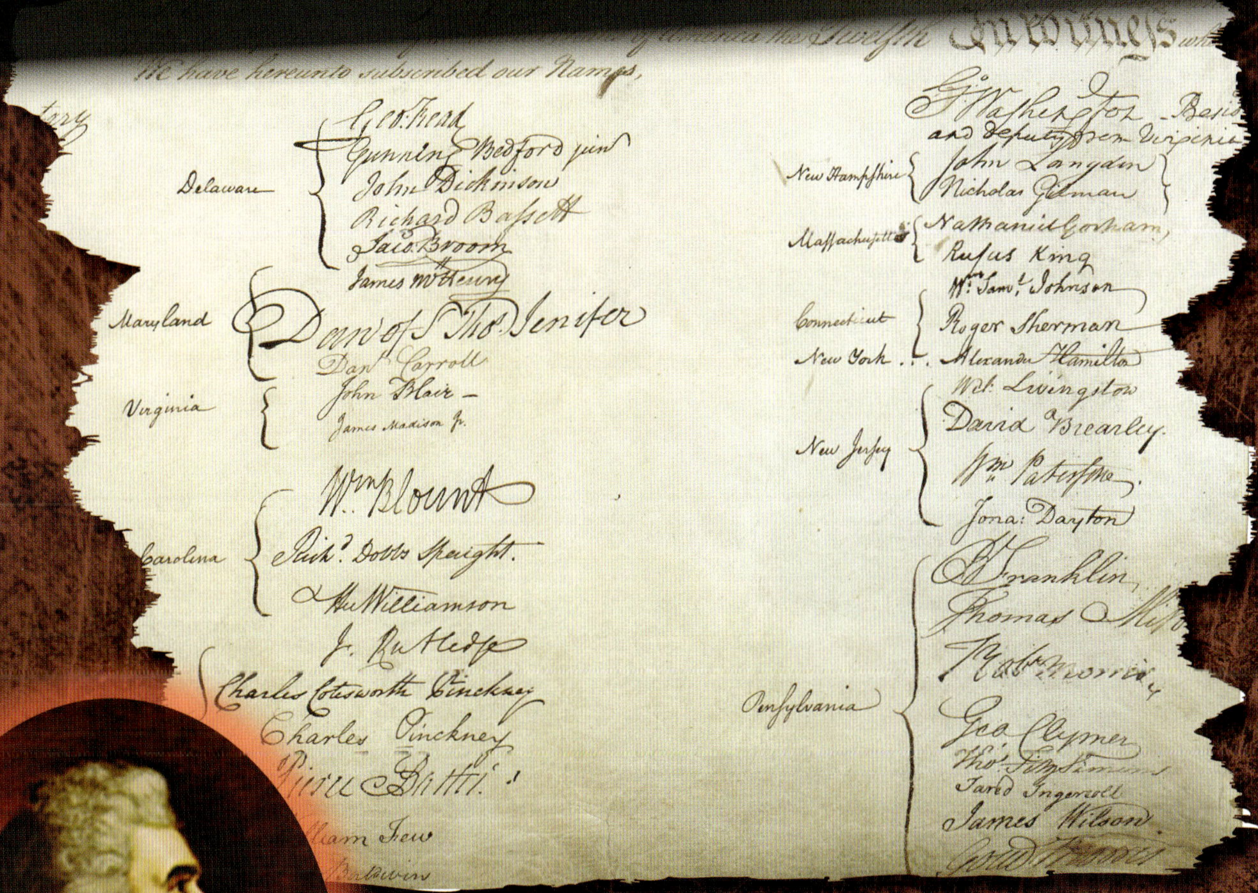

JONATHAN DAYTON

YOUNGEST AND OLDEST

Benjamin Franklin was the oldest delegate to sign the Constitution. He was 81 at the time. The youngest delegate was Jonathan Dayton of New Jersey. He was 26.

AFTER THE CONVENTION

THE MYTH: ALL THE STATES WERE HAPPY ABOUT THE CONSTITUTION AND QUICKLY SIGNED IT.

THE FACTS:

The Framers agreed that only nine of the 13 states needed to **ratify** the document. It wasn't easy, though.

A group called the Federalists thought the Constitution was nearly perfect. Others, called Anti-Federalists, thought it made the federal government too strong. They worried about states' and people's rights. Federalists promised a bill of rights would be added to the Constitution. Knowing the federal government's powers would be limited eased some people's fears about the Constitution.

These were some of the Founding Fathers on both sides of the Constitution debate, or argument.

JOHN JAY
FEDERALIST

JAMES MADISON
FEDERALIST

ALEXANDER HAMILTON
FEDERALIST

PATRICK HENRY
ANTI-FEDERALIST

JAMES MONROE
ANTI-FEDERALIST

SAMUEL ADAMS
ANTI-FEDERALIST

Some states ratified the Constitution quickly. Others debated for a long time. Finally, New Hampshire became the ninth state to ratify it in June 1788, making it law.

George Washington became the first president of the United States on April 30, 1789. North Carolina and Rhode Island hadn't even ratified the Constitution yet! Rhode Island was the last to ratify it in May 1790.

Even today, people debate about new amendments to the Constitution. The true story of the US Constitution hasn't ended yet!

A DIFFERENT THANKSGIVING DAY

President George Washington asked everyone to give thanks for the country's new constitution on November 26, 1789.

SIGNING THE CONSTITUTION

A TIMELINE OF THE CONSTITUTIONAL CONVENTION

MAY 25, 1787
THE CONSTITUTIONAL CONVENTION STARTS IN PHILADELPHIA, PENNSYLVANIA.

SEPTEMBER 17, 1787
DELEGATES SIGN THE CONSTITUTION.

DECEMBER 7, 1787
DELAWARE IS THE FIRST STATE TO RATIFY THE CONSTITUTION.

JUNE 21, 1788
NEW HAMPSHIRE IS THE NINTH STATE TO RATIFY THE CONSTITUTION.

MARCH 4, 1789
CONGRESS NAMES THIS DATE TO BEGIN THE NEW GOVERNMENT UNDER THE CONSTITUTION.

APRIL 30, 1789
GEORGE WASHINGTON BECOMES THE FIRST PRESIDENT OF THE UNITED STATES.

SEPTEMBER 25, 1789
THE BILL OF RIGHTS PASSES IN CONGRESS.

MAY 29, 1790
RHODE ISLAND IS THE LAST STATE TO RATIFY THE CONSTITUTION.

GLOSSARY

ambassador: an official representative of a government

amendment: a change made to the US Constitution

compromise: a way of reaching an agreement in which each person or group gives up something that was wanted in order to end an argument

convention: a large meeting of people who come to a place to talk about their shared work or to make decisions as a group

document: an official paper

economy: the process or system by which goods and services are produced, sold, and bought in a region

engraving: a picture made by cutting into metal or wood, inking the surface of the metal or wood, and pressing paper against it

minority: the group that is the smaller part of a larger group

miracle: a very amazing or unusual event, thing, or achievement

myth: an idea or story that is believed by many people but that is not true

proposal: something put forward for consideration or acceptance

ratify: to make a treaty or agreement official by signing it or voting for it

representative: someone who acts or speaks for or in support of another person or group

FOR MORE INFORMATION

BOOKS

Manger, Katherine. *The U.S. Constitution.* New York, NY: Britannica Educational Publishing, 2017.

Ransom, Candice. *Who Wrote the U.S. Constitution? And Other Questions About the Constitutional Convention of 1787.* Minneapolis, MN: Lerner Publications, 2011.

Schmidt, Maegan. *The US Constitution and Bill of Rights.* Minneapolis, MN: ABDO Publishing Company, 2013.

WEBSITES

Congress for Kids: Introduction to the Constitution
www.congressforkids.net/Constitution_index.htm
Travel back in time and find out the facts about the people who wrote the Constitution.

The National Constitution Center
constitutioncenter.org
Learn all about the creation of the Constitution of the United States. Read an interactive version of the Constitution.

INDEX

13th Amendment 15
15th Amendment 16
19th Amendment 16
26th Amendment 16
"all men are created equal" 18
amendments 5, 28
Anti-Federalists 26
Articles of Confederation 6
Bill of Rights 5, 13, 24, 26, 29
Dayton, Jonathan 25
federal government 6, 8, 10, 26
Federalists 26
Founding Fathers 10, 27
Framers 7, 8, 11, 14, 22, 24, 26
Franklin, Benjamin 10, 11, 25
Jefferson, Thomas 12, 13
Madison, James 12, 13, 22, 23
New Hampshire 18, 28, 29
Philadelphia, Pennsylvania 4, 7, 29
republic 20, 21
Rhode Island 8, 9, 28, 29
right to vote 16
slavery 14, 15
slaves 14, 15
Virginia Plan 22
Washington, George 9, 11, 23, 28, 29
"We the People" 18, 19